# UFOS THROUGH TIME

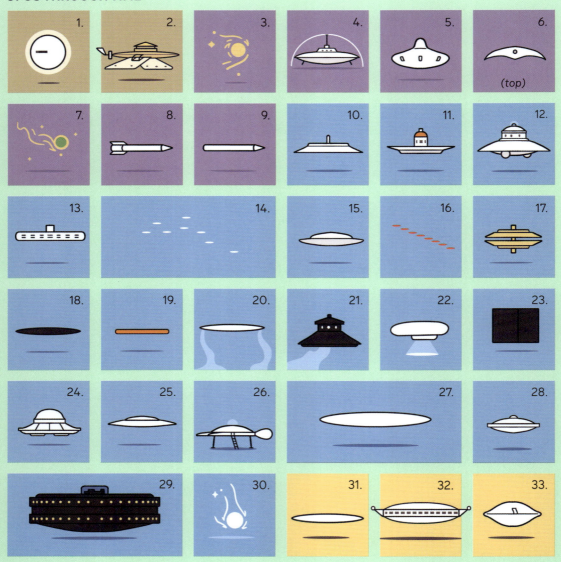

## 1800s

1. Hull, UK, (1801)
2. Sacramento, USA (1896)

## 1940s

3. Worldwide, (1940s)
4. Ängelholm, Sweden, (1946)
5. Bauru, Brazil, (1947)
6. Mt. Rainer, USA (1947)
7. Around USA, (1948)
8. Around Sweden, (1940s)
9. Fukuoka, Japan, (1948)

## 1950s

10. Sheridan, USA, (1950)
11. Epu Pel, Argentina, (1950)
12. Mt. Palomar, USA (1952)
13. Hasselbach, E. Germany, (1952)
14. Washington D.C., USA (1952)
15. Oldenburg, W. Germany, (1952)
16. Norfolk, USA, (1952)
17. Castel Franco, Italy, (1952)
18. Agoura, USA, (1953)
19. Pto. Maldonado, Peru, (1954)
20. Manbhum, India, (1954)
21. Smethwick, UK, (1954)
22. Melborne, Australia, (1954)
23. Ombues, Argentina, (1956)
24. Bexley, UK, (1955)
25. Drakensberg, S. Africa, (1956)
26. Minas Gerais, Brazil, (1957)
27. Baltimore, USA, (1958)
28. Trindade, Brazil, (1959)
29. Blenheim, New Zealand, (1959)
30. Walworth, USA, (1959)

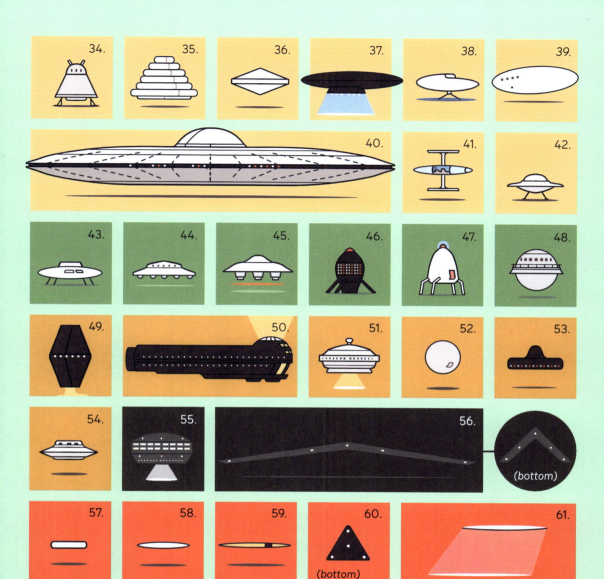

## 1960s

31. Victoria, Canada, (1960)
32. Lancaster, USA, (1961)
33. Eagle River, USA, (1961)
34. Parr, UK, (1963)
35. Stanton, USA, (1964)
36. Merlin, USA, (1964)
37. Sunnyvale, USA, (1964)
38. Valensole, France, (1965)
39. Reboullion, France, (1966)
40. Vietnam, (1966)
41. Réunion Island, (1968)
42. Pirassununga, Brazil, (1969)

## 1970s

43. Kinnula, Finland, (1971)
44. Skipton, UK, (1978)
45. Charleston, USA, (1978)
46. Gerena, Spain, (1978)
47. Mindalore, South Africa, (1978)
48. Dechmont, UK, (1979)

## 1980s

49. Dayton, USA, (1980)
50. Mobile, USA, (1983)
51. Gulf Breeze, USA, (1987)
52. Voronezh, USSR, (1989)
53. Duclair, France, (1989)
54. Groom Lake, NV, USA (1989)

## 1990s

55. Yukon, Canada, (1996)
56. Phoenix, Arizona, (1997)

## 2000s

57. San Diego Coast, USA, (2004)
58. Chicago, USA, (2006)
59. French Coast, (2007)
60. West Midlands, UK, (2007)
61. Hangzhou, China, (2010)

To those I have annoyed with endless chatter about UFOs,
for the folk at Flying Eye for joining in on the fun,
to David Clarke for his expertise, and lastly,
to the Greys from Zeta Reticuli; fly safely.

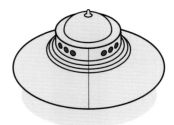

This edition first published by Flying Eye Books in 2025 from material originally published in
*An Illustrated History of UFOs* by Adam Allsuch Boardman (Nobrow press, 2020).
www.flyingeyebooks.com

Represented by: Authorised Rep Compliance Ltd.
Ground Floor, 71 Lower Baggot Street, Dublin, D02 P593, Ireland
www.arccompliance.com

Text and illustrations © Adam Allsuch Boardman 2020

Original Content Consultant: Hayley Stevens

Adam Allsuch Boardman has asserted his right under the Copyright, Designs
and Patents Act, 1988, to be identified as the Author and Illustrator of this Work.

All rights reserved. No part of this publication may be reproduced or transmitted in any form or
by any means, electronic or mechanical, including photocopying, recording or by any information
and storage retrieval system, without prior written consent from the publisher.

1 3 5 7 9 10 8 6 4 2

ISBN: 978-1-83874-947-7

Published in the USA by Flying Eye Books Ltd.
Printed in China on FSC® certified paper.

# THE UNEXPLAINED

ADAM ALLSUCH BOARDMAN

*FLYING EYE BOOKS*

# CONTENTS

Flanders, Belgium, 1972

# Introduction — 8

## Before UFOs — 10
Ancient astronauts
Mythic visitors
Spirits from space
Mystery airships
Foo Fighters
The War of the Worlds

## The 1940s — 22
Flying saucers
Saucers attack!
The Roswell incident
The Men in Black
Government gets involved
The Bermuda Triangle

## The 1950s — 34
Coming of the contactees
UFOs over the Pacific
Giant Rock Spacecraft Convention

## The 1960s — 42
The Hill abduction
Identified flying objects
Civilian UFO associations
The Kecksburg incident

## The 1970s — 52
Close encounters
The Travis Walton incident
Is Bigfoot an alien?
The Petrozavodsk incident
Crop circles

## The 1980s — 64
Caught on camera
The Rendlesham Forest incident
In deep water
Area 51

## The 1990s — 76
The Phoenix lights

## 21st Century — 80
Government disclosure
The Pentagon's saucer search
SETI
Ufology today

## Glossary — 90

## Index — 92

# INTRODUCTION

Throughout history, people have witnessed the spectacle of strange objects in the sky. Whether they are alien interlopers or strange weather, they've always been mysterious enough to cause government investigations, create secretive societies and dedicated investigators.

In the 1950s, The United States Airforce decided to give these strange flying objects a name: 'Unidentified Flying Objects' (UFOs). People who study them are called 'ufologists'.

When most people think of UFOs, they imagine flying saucers with green aliens inside. But that's just one idea among many, and it's commonly argued that aliens are usually not green at all!

This book is full of exciting stories about close encounters, research and conspiracy theories to inspire anyone interested in UFOs to learn more and spend some time looking up at the sky.

I have always been interested in UFOs since I was a child, reading books about them in bookstores. In writing this book, I eagerly dove back into the world of conspiratorial cork boards, books and online research.

Ufology is full of fun theories (and debates about which of them is true!) and my greatest hope is that you may go on to find your own truth, which is, after all, *out there*.

# COMMON UFO SHAPES

Anomalous light

Adamski-type

Dirigible

Light formation

Cigar

Saturn shape

Flying saucer

Sports model

Conical hat

Boomerang

Egg with landing gear

Triangle

# BEFORE UFOS

# ANCIENT ASTRONAUTS

**Humans have always been fascinated by space. Our ancestors built megaliths to align with the stars and planets and etched drawings of the sky on rocks and bones. Ancient explorers like the Polynesians and Vikings used the stars as a map to guide them to distant lands.**

But what if the cosmos returned the interest? Some believe aliens visited ancient humanity, providing them with useful advice such as how to build cities and sow crops. The theory was proposed by the book *Chariots of the Gods?* (1968) written by Swiss hotel manager Erich von Däniken. The book alleges that mega-structures such as the Egyptian pyramids or the vast Nazca lines in Peru are evidence of extraterrestrial assistance, and of interaction between humans and aliens, who posed as gods.

Critics of this idea argue that it makes people look down on ancient civilisations by suggesting that they couldn't have earned their achievements without help. Instead, their success actually came from thousands of years of hard work and progress.

## False Findings

The items on this page supposedly depict aliens, or show engineering knowledge beyond the reach of our ancestors.

Supporters of the ancient astronaut hypothesis believe that these kinds of artefacts are evidence of alien intelligence. As interesting as this might be, this encourages a disrespectful view of our ancestors, their rich cultural histories and impressive craftsmanship.

### Key
1. The Pyramids, Egypt
2. Stonehenge, UK
3. Shakoki-dogu figurine, Japan
4. Hieroglyphs, Egypt
5. Cave painting, Algeria
6. Petroglyph, USA
7. Moai, Easter Island
8. Antikythera mechanism, Greece
9. Mayan engraving, Mexico
10. Iron pillar, India
11. Quimbaya artefact, Colombia
12. Cave drawing, Italy
13. Painting, Serbia
14. Incan walls, Peru
15. The Nazca lines, Peru

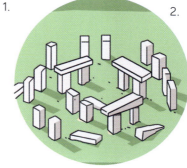

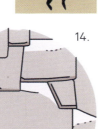
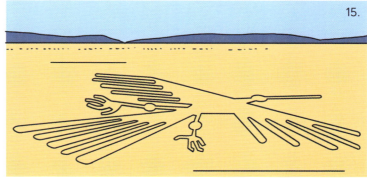

# MYTHIC VISITORS

Most cultures have their fair share of tales warning of færies, goblins and trickster spirits. While many consider the stories to be folk tales or myths, some believe they are accounts of actual alien encounters.

### Middle Eastern god-aliens
In 1976, Russian author Zecharia Sitchin proposed that the Anunnaki, ancient Mesopotamian deities, were alien beings. In his books, Sitchin told of how the Anunnaki enslaved the human race for the purposes of extracting gold. These god-aliens returned to the planet Nibiru during the ice age and this is where they presumably continue to plot against us.

## Færie

European folklore frequently makes reference to mysterious other realms such as the land of 'færie'. Creatures from this realm, also called færies, are said to enter our world and kidnap unsuspecting humans. Some ufologists believe these stories stem from historic alien abductions.

## Green children

In 12th century England, two odd siblings appeared in the village of Woolpit and astonished locals with their green hue. The younger child, a boy, died of sickness but the girl lived in the village for many years. Some suggest that the children were aliens left on Earth by some tragic circumstance.

## Will-o'-the-Wisp

Will-o'-the-Wisps (meaning a torch that moves by itself) appear in folk stories across many cultures, from the Americas to East Asia. They are small, ghostly lights with the mischievous intent of drawing travellers from the road. **Skeptics** suggest the wisps are visions caused by **swamp gas** or ergot poisoning from dodgy bread.

## Cities in the sky

In the 19th century, locals in Orkney, UK and Finland reportedly saw cities floating in the sky. US prospector Richard Willoughby claimed to have a photo of one such city above Alaska in 1899, but the picture was later found to depict a foggy day in Bristol, UK.

# SPIRITS FROM SPACE

During the 19th century, spiritualism became incredibly popular in the West. The movement centred around the belief that the spirit world could be contacted through parlour activities (party games) or a 'medium' (a psychic person).

Mediums claimed contact not only with earthly spirits, but also entities from other planets. During the 19th century, this usually meant Mars or Venus, as knowledge of more distant worlds was limited.

**Medium to the Martians**
Well-known American medium Vesta La Viesta (a pseudonym) gave many lectures in the early 1900s on her experiences of communing with Martians and Venusians through astral projection (the ability to move one's soul independent of the body).

### Fun for the whole family

'Talking boards' such as the Ouija board were mass-produced from the 1890s, allowing any spiritual enthusiast to participate. Mass production might show that people used to be more open to paranormal concepts, accepting things that we might find hard to believe today.

### Crowley's contact

British 'wizard' Aleister Crowley claimed to have made telepathic contacts during magic rituals. One such contact, in 1917, was with an entity named 'Lam'. Luckily, Crowley later illustrated this entity, which looks strikingly like a **'grey'** alien (this was some decades before it became a popular image).

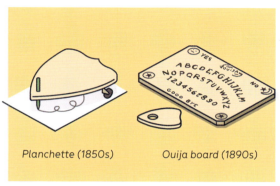
Planchette (1850s)    Ouija board (1890s)

### Staging the supernatural

The magician Harry Houdini exposed many mediums as frauds who took advantage of people's grief for money and publicity. Techniques used by mediums included concealed strings to create the effect of levitation, extending grabbers for 'ghostly touches' and hidden music boxes for unearthly sounds.

# MYSTERY AIRSHIPS

Towards the end of 1896, mysterious airships were sighted around California, USA. Mass sightings continued the next year across North America. These **flaps (a period of many sightings)** made excellent newspaper content. After compiling witness statements, some reporters suggested the airships may have arrived from Mars or Venus. The excitement over these airships may show how the new genre of science fiction influenced sightings.

Science fiction writers like Jules Verne and H.G. Wells wrote tales of airships and submarines, highlighting the public's fear of growing industrial progress.

# FOO FIGHTERS

Preceding and during the Second World War, some pilots noticed peculiar lights near their planes. These were named **'Foo Fighters'** by the Allies, in reference to a popular comic strip.

## Wonder weapons?
The US 415th Night Fighter Squadron had several encounters with the Foo Fighters, and on one occasion chased a formation of orange fireballs, only to watch them eerily disappear as if turned off by a switch. Some suspected that Foo Fighters were secret weapons.

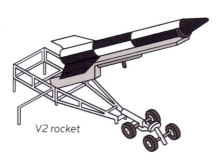

*V2 rocket*

## Weird weather
After the war, St. Elmo's fire was commonly pointed to as the source of Foo Fighters. St. Elmo's fire is a weather phenomena that sometimes occurs in stormy conditions. When the air around pointy objects like wings or masts ionises, it can glow. The effect has been documented on modern aircraft, creating a web of harmless plasma around planes.

# THE WAR OF THE WORLDS

On 30th October 1938, the Mercury Theatre in New York broadcast a play on CBS radio based on H.G. Wells's *The War of the Worlds* (1898). Directed and narrated by Orson Welles, the play was made to sound like a real news broadcast about Martians invading Earth.

### Mass hysteria

After people believed that the alien invasion was real, reporters chased down the Mercury Theatre members and CBS staff, forcing Welles to apologise publically.

## Pre-war panic

Historians argue that the panic wasn't as big as reported and that CBS and newspapers exaggerated the chaos – it made fun news during a time when Europe was about to plunge itself into woeful war. Either way, it shows how eagerly the public engaged with the idea of alien visitors.

# THE 1940s

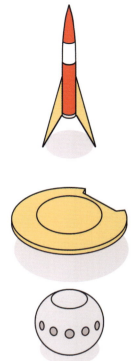

# FLYING SAUCERS

The modern history of UFOs is widely agreed to begin with the events of June 24th, 1947. On this particular day, Kenneth Arnold, a trader in fire safety equipment, observed something that would initiate the age of flying saucers. At around 3pm, Arnold was flying his CallAir plane near Mt. Rainer in Washington state, US when he saw nine distant objects. Arnold vividly described the things as 'shaped like a pie-plate' and 'saucer-like' in their movement. When he reported his story to the press, they created the term 'flying saucer'.

## A cultural icon

Sensing the potential for another sensational scoop, editor Raymond Palmer (of Shaver Mystery fame) contacted Arnold and asked to buy the story for his magazine, but Arnold happily gave an account for free. The issue's cover included an imaginative illustration of three flying saucers above Arnold's plane, establishing the flying saucer as a symbol of otherworldliness, associated with the UFO phenomenon.

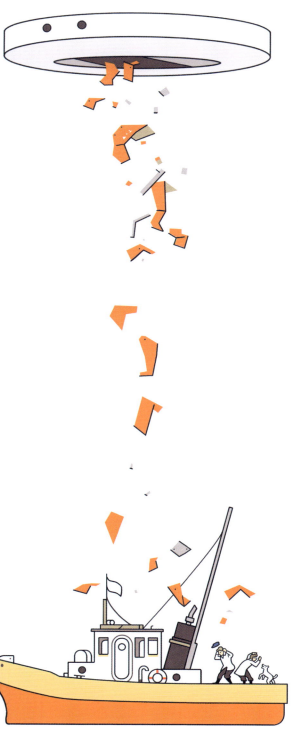

*Flying Saucer*

*View from beneath*

# SAUCERS ATTACK!

After great public interest in Arnold's flying saucer sighting, Palmer sought similar stories for his new magazine, *Fate*. Learning of a similar sighting on Maury Island, he sent Arnold as a investigative journalist. He met with a pair of harbour workers who claimed that six doughnut-shaped craft had flown over their boat and dropped weird metal on them, killing a dog and injuring a young man.

One worker, Harold Dahl, claimed that a mysterious dark-suited man visited his trailer after the sighting and warned him not to share his tale, this being an early example of the **'Men in Black'** legend.

Arnold excitedly called upon two US Air Force officers to take a look at the unusual metal left behind by the UFO. Upon arrival, the officers were quick to note that it was simply luminium. In a hurry to get back to base for the next day, the officers took a flight in the early hours, but tragically died when the plane crashed, fuelling wild conspiracies involving a government cover-up.

CLOSE ENCOUNTERS

# THE ROSWELL INCIDENT

Shortly after Kenneth Arnold's flying saucer sighting in June 1947, a rancher named William 'Mac' Brazel found the debris from a crashed object near Roswell, New Mexico. Brazel thought the debris, mostly foil and rods, was curious. Once he reported his find in town, soldiers from the Roswell Army Air Field (RAAF) quickly arrived to take the damaged detritus. The RAAF issued a press release on 8th July, announcing that they had indeed recovered a 'flying disc'!

Mac Brazel discovers debris

The RAAF announce they have recovered a 'flying disc'

**Myths and legends**
Details of the crashed spaceship, including dead aliens and the presence of the Men in Black passed into popular culture thanks to the book *The Roswell Incident* (1980). The book was based on witness interviews gathered by authors Charles Berlitz and William Moore (helped by famous Canadian ufologist Stanton Friedman).

## Project Mogul

The day after Brazel's discovery, the RAAF issued a correction: the recovered debris belonged to a **weather balloon** and not an alien spaceship. Historians now believe the reason for the rushed excuse was to conceal the testing of secret 'Project Mogul', a monitoring balloon used to spy on Russian atom bomb tests.

Men in Black

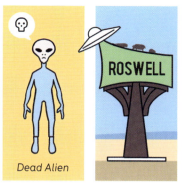
Dead Alien

## Saucer sightseeing

Whether it was a balloon or spaceship debris in 1947, Roswell has established itself as the spiritual capital of UFOs, with museums, themed restaurants, bars and highly inventive merchandise. Its name has become associated with themes of conspiracy, cover-up and aliens.

# THE MEN IN BLACK

The Men in Black (MiB) are said to be the dedicated shadows of UFO witnesses. Although making their debut as far back in the 1940s, the myth was largely popularised by American author Gray Barker's book *They Knew too Much About Flying Saucers* (1953). Barker's book described strangers arriving at the homes of saucer enthusiasts to ask strange questions and make sinister threats.

**Funky phantoms**
Witnesses have described the Men in Black as tall and unusually pale. Their faces are often gaunt and hairless, with lipstick applied to their thin, expressionless lips. To the general public, the MiB are most commonly associated with the *Men in Black* film franchise, in which they are depicted more like fun space cops than messengers of terror.

# GOVERNMENT GETS INVOLVED

The US Airforce (USAF) began investigating UFOs in 1948. Their aims were to manage public interest, debunk cases and learn whether UFOs might be Soviet spy planes. Project Blue Book was their longest and best known project.

Air Force investigations were often motivated by the fact their own personnel kept seeing UFOs around military bases.

Project Blue Book staff

**1 Discover the truth**
The first USAF project, **Project Sign** concluded in 1949 with a report called *Estimate of the Situation*, which outlined the remaining mystery of UFOs and entertained the possibility that some UFOs were spaceships piloted by aliens.

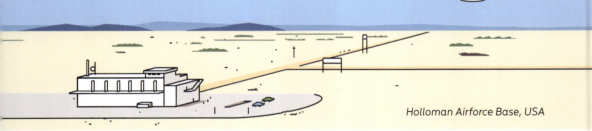
Holloman Airforce Base, USA

Alabama skies, USA, 24 July 1948

**2 Deny everything**
Dissatisfied with remaining questions, USAF leadership launched the second project, **Project Grudge** in 1949. Grudge sought to focus on debunking sightings and in August 1949, the Grudge Report stated that no UFO was beyond explanation and hoped that would end the affair.

### ③ See both sides

**Project Blue Book** had a lasting impact on the UFO community as it introduced a lot of terminology and processes still used to this day. This investigation began in March 1952. Under the leadership of Captain Edward Ruppelt, the project hoped to provide more balanced assessment and apply a more scientific approach. Perhaps the most lasting impression has been made by the term 'UFO', created during the project.

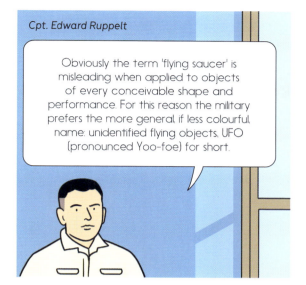

*Cpt. Edward Ruppelt*

Obviously the term 'flying saucer' is misleading when applied to objects of every conceivable shape and performance. For this reason the military prefers the more general, if less colourful, name: unidentified flying objects, UFO (pronounced Yoo-foe) for short.

### Capital craziness

After the significant flap of UFO reports in December 1952 centred around Washington DC, the CIA started a review of Project Blue Book. This 'Robertson Panel' formed in January 1953 and concluded the government should focus on proving what's not true instead of guessing, which led the UFO community and journalists to believe the military was hiding the 'truth'.

### Learned legacy

Astronomer J. Allen Hynek gained several decades of experience while consulting on USAF projects designed to explain UFOs. After the closure of Blue Book in 1969, he continued to be very active in ufology and set up the Centre for UFO Studies (CUFOS) in Illinois, USA.

# THE BERMUDA TRIANGLE

In the study of the paranormal, many investigators have identified places in the world that seem to attract strange events. One famous example is the Bermuda Triangle, an area in the Atlantic Ocean where planes and ships seem to go missing in unusual ways.

Those who have survived their encounters with the Triangle report compasses going haywire, electrical fog, ghost ships and lights under the sea. Theorists have suggested many explanations, such as time anomalies, technology from the lost city of Atlantis, and interference by flying saucers. Ufologists such as John Spencer and M.K. Jessup concluded that the Bermuda Triangle is plagued by malevolent aliens. They alleged that both planes and ships were drawn away from their correct paths by flying saucers, in a similar manner to færies misleading travellers in folklore.

### Santa Maria, 1492
Shortly before making landfall in the Bahamas, the logs of the *Santa Maria* describe how the crew witnessed a ghostly light over the ocean waves, and later odd compass behaviour.

### Carroll A. Deering, 1912
The schooner *Carroll A. Deering* was found abandoned just outside the Bermuda Triangle. The crew, lifeboats and provisions were missing but no clear reason could be discovered for the ship's abandonment.

### Flight 19, 1949
In 1945, five US Navy planes, 'Flight 19', disappeared without a trace when training off the coast of Florida. Radio calls to base suggested an eerie interference; they had trouble navigating with compasses and couldn't spot familiar islands below. Radio contact was soon cut by poor weather, making their fate a mystery.

### Time tunnel, 1976
While flying to Florida, Bruce Gernon and his father encountered a strange cloud. According to the Gernons, flying into the vapour revealed it to be a long tunnel filled with strange light. Upon exiting, they contacted air traffic control and found that they had arrived in half the usual time!

# COMING OF THE CONTACTEES

Growing public interest in UFOs in the early 1950s created a new variety of celebrity. Like spirit mediums before them, some people claimed they had talked with ambassadors from another world, except rather than the spirit world, these visitors came from space.

### Alien encounters
In 1952, Polish-American George Adamski, who called himself a spiritual teacher, claimed he was visited by flying saucers and a friendly alien named Orthon. Adamski detailed his encounters in his best-selling book *Flying Saucers Have Landed* (1953). The book was almost entirely written by Desmond Leslie. Over time, Adamski's story was retold with changes, but it's important because it helped popularise the character of the 'nordic' alien.

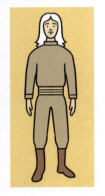 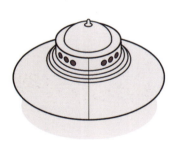  

### Alien archetype
Before the popular idea of aliens being short and grey, otherworldly visitors were typically reported to be light-haired folk in skin-tight suits. Initially they were referred to as 'Space Brothers', while today 'Nordic' is more commonly used. Orthon apparently made warnings about impending nuclear threat, but offered little practical advice.

### Official intrigue
Project Blue Book's director Edward Ruppelt decided to visit Adamski after receiving many letters asking for an investigation of his story. Ruppelt found Adamski odd, and noted in his UFO reports that more and more contactees were tricking vulnerable people out of money.

### The Adamski Type
Adamski's book included blurry pictures of the alien craft, which critics believed looked just like part of a gasoline lamp. Regardless, the 'Adamski Type' flying saucer became a well-known image, thanks in part to the fantastic cover illustration of Adamski's book.

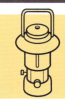  
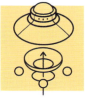  

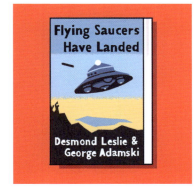

*Scout Ship*

*Mother Ship*

### A change in the wind
The arrival of contactees like Adamski marked a change in the tone of UFO history. As many people laughed at those claiming to have met 'space brothers', ufologists struggled to be taken seriously.

# UFOS OVER THE PACIFIC

UFOs were seen not just in America but all over the world, leading different countries to start their own investigations.

Rockhampton, Australia, 14th August 1952

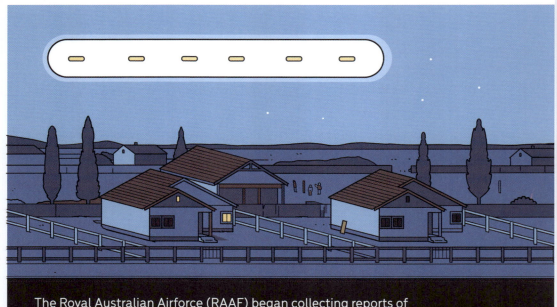

The Royal Australian Airforce (RAAF) began collecting reports of UFOs in the early 1950s. The organisation gave simple, uninteresting explanations for sightings when questioned by press.

Malvern, Australia, May 1953

## The Drury Affair

One case in 1953 drew particular press attention due the footage captured by aviation official Tom Drury.

Drury observed and filmed what he described as a guided missile. The footage was passed around various government departments and to the US for analysis. UFO enthusiasts purchased prints of the footage and were supremely disappointed by their quality, which prompted some to suspect there had been a cover-up.

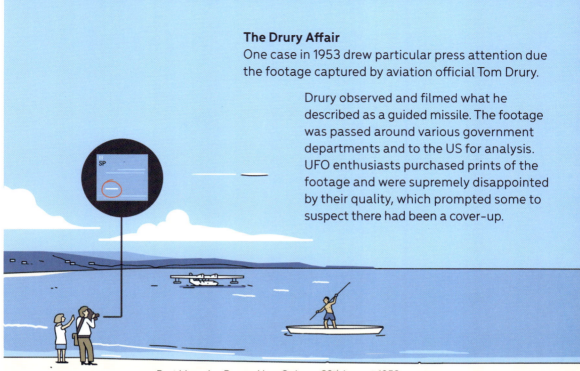

Port Moresby, Papua New Guinea, 23rd August 1953

## Delightful disclosure

In 1982, ufologists were delighted to be granted access to the RAAF's UFO files. The files, now gathered and studied by many UFO historians, allow us to see the exchanges between officials and civilian groups. Responding to demands for an investigation of 'The Father Gill Sighting' (a missionary in Papua New Guinea saw aliens waving from a flying saucer) officials dryly suggested the event was 'probably... natural phenomena'.

To the disappointment of some believers, disclosures such as this reveal a dull truth — militaries know just as little about UFOs as the general public. That's probably why many people prefer more exciting conspiracy theories.

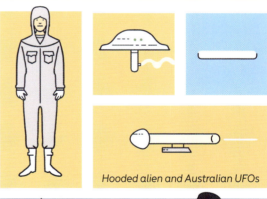

Hooded alien and Australian UFOs

# GIANT ROCK SPACECRAFT CONVENTION

As UFOs became a popular topic of speculation, partly due to science fiction books and films, a group of people began to believe they came from outer space. Starting in 1953, American aircraft mechanic and contactee George Van Tassel hosted the annual 'Giant Rock Spacecraft Convention' at his airfield in California.

*The Integratron*

## Community gathering
The convention was an important exchange of UFO ideas, mostly supporting the belief that UFOs were extraterrestrial. Thousands of people attended until the 1970s to hear talks and buy the latest UFO books. The event continued to attract guests until Van Tassel's death in 1978, after which other conventions started to form their own communities.

## A home for meditation
Not far from the convention ground Van Tassel built a structure called 'The Integratron'. The build was funded largely by donations. It was believed to help with meditation and even cure illnesses, and it is still open today.

# THE 1960S

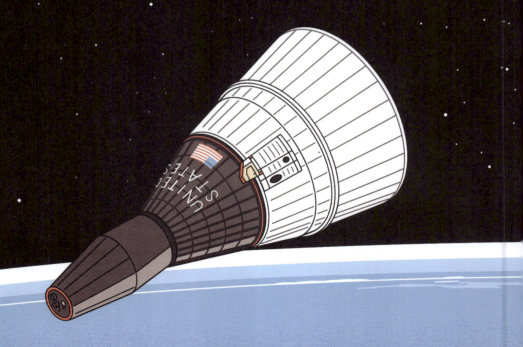

Earth's orbit, June 1965

ABDUCTIONS

# THE HILL ABDUCTION

The 1960s were a booming time for UFO phenomenon, with famous abduction cases and mass sightings. Meanwhile, official government investigations did little to reduce public interest or fully explain UFO activity.

**An interrupted journey**
The most well-known **abductee** incident concerns the American couple Betty and Barney Hill. On 19th September 1961, the Hills were driving back from a holiday when they spotted a flying saucer. Having studied the craft closely, they left with a sense of unease. When the Hills returned home they had the unusual impression that they had forgotten something important.

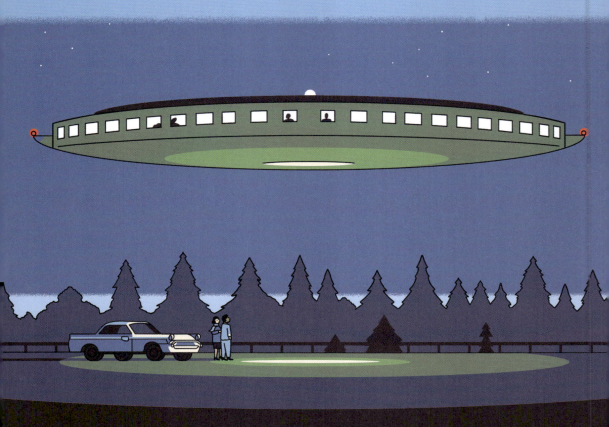

## Making a report

Betty telephoned Pease Airforce Base to report the sighting. The officers decided the couple had misidentified Jupiter.

## Betty does her research

Still eager to make sense of what the two of them had seen, Betty borrowed a UFO book from the library by Major Donald Keyhoe – director of the civilian UFO research group NICAP – and decided to write to him about her experience.

*Donald Keyhoe, director of NICAP*

## Missing time

In response to Betty's letter, NICAP investigators visited the Hills and found them to be a delightful and honest couple. They noted that the Hill's drive home had taken much longer than it should have and estimated that the couple had misplaced *seven* hours after the encounter!

An element of 'missing time' has been noted across many abduction accounts. Some ufologists attribute it to a deliberate attempt by the alien abductors to remove memories of the abduction.

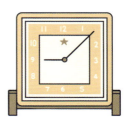

# IDENTIFIED FLYING OBJECTS

Throughout the 1960s, the US Air Force's Project Blue Book continued to debunk UFOs with increasingly creative explanations for the press, often making extra effort to avoid suggesting aliens were involved. One infamous explanation was to blame sightings on 'swamp gas'.

LENTICULAR CLOUD

REFLECTIVE BIRDS

SWAMP GAS

PLANET

SHOOTING STAR

AURORA BOREALIS

BALL LIGHTNING

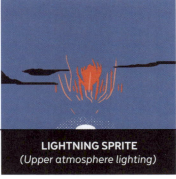
LIGHTNING SPRITE
(Upper atmosphere lighting)

ST. ELMO'S FIRE
(See: Foo Fighters p.19)

## Ambiguous aircraft

Meanwhile, the **Cold War** between America and the Soviet Union quietly raged on. An arms race of hi-tech aircraft escalated, and modern ufologists believe that these were responsible for a great many sightings.

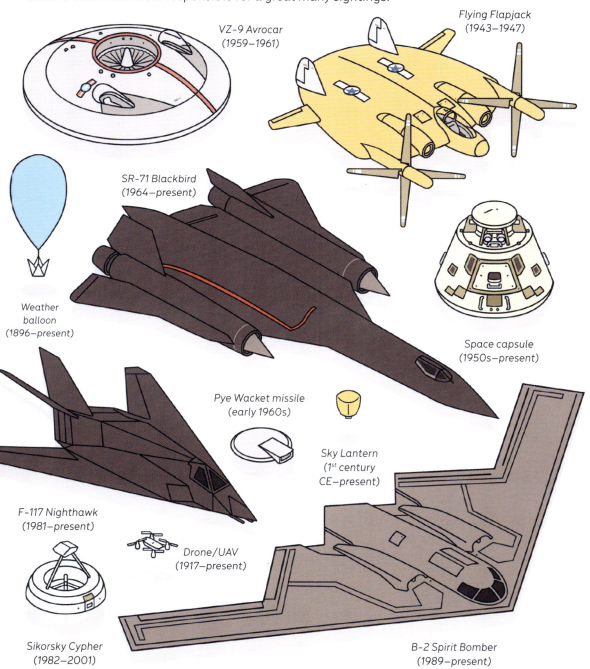

# CIVILIAN UFO ASSOCIATIONS

**Outside of official government and military interest in the matter, many civilian and amateur groups were forming as public interest in UFOs swelled in the 1950s and 60s.**

Members of associations were largely just curious people with an interest in learning more about the mystery.

UFO associations were usually reliant on donations and subscriptions to their journals (and thus were often short on money). UFO journals reported on recent sightings, and printed the latest photos as well as reader letters.

### NICAP
The American 'National Investigations Committee On Aerial Phenomena' (NICAP) formed in 1954. It attracted UFO enthusiasts who were open-minded but not certain that UFOs were aliens. To avoid being ridiculed, NICAP investigators avoided exploring alien abductions or sightings. NICAP suffered from money troubles until dissolving in the 1980s.

### BUFORA
In 1962, the 'British UFO Research Association' (BUFORA) formed to bring together various UFO groups, known as 'Saucer Clubs', across the UK. BUFORA remains active to this day.

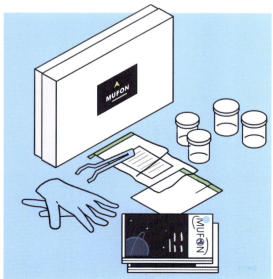

### MUFON
The American group 'Mutual UFO Network' (MUFON) was formed in 1969. Many of their members were frustrated with the government's dismissive attitude towards UFOs. In the early 1970s, MUFON began releasing field manuals to help investigations. Today, they offer paid membership that gives exclusive access to their archives. MUFON is still one of the largest civilian UFO investigation organisations.

**CLOSE ENCOUNTERS**

# THE KECKSBURG INCIDENT

On the evening of 9th December 1965, a strange object allegedly smashed into the Kecksburg woodland in Pennsylvania, US. The press reported that a thorough search had found no trace of any fallen object.

On 19th September 1990, an episode of television series *Unsolved Mysteries* rekindled interest in the story, and alleged that the fallen object had actually been an acorn-shaped spacecraft that was quickly smuggled away by the US military.

**NASA findings**
Searching for the truth in the 2000s, journalist Leslie Kean forced NASA to share hundreds of files. Kean's hope was that the files would unearth proof that a space object had been taken from Kecksburg for secretive study. Disappointingly, the files did not unveil a shadowy conspiracy, but did contain some mention of NASA providing consultation on other UFO incidents.

## Satellite or super-weapon?
Skeptics generally agree that witnesses to the Kecksburg event probably saw part of a fallen satellite or meteor being whisked away by the USAF. However, The History Channel's imaginatively named documentary 'Nazi UFO Conspiracy' proposed that the acorn-shaped object was actually a flying saucer built by Nazis. The story goes that the USAF secured the craft at the end of WW2 but can't get it to fly without crashing into the woods

# THE 1970S

*Pascagoula, USA, 20th October 1973*

# CLOSE ENCOUNTERS

Project Blue Book's Professor J. Allen Hynek published his book *The UFO Experience* in 1972, explaining his method for organising UFO reports. His system, known as the 'Hynek Scale' or the 'Close Encounters' system, is still used by UFO researchers today.

J. Allen Hynek

### 1
**Night lights**
The most common and least strange UFOs: lights in the night sky.

### 2
**Daylight discs**
UFOs seen in the daytime. These are most commonly discs or saucers.

### 3
**Radar-Visual**
A visual encounter corroborated with **RADAR** contact.

### Heroic Hynek
Hynek's work in ufology continues to inspire others in the field. Rather than promoting alien conspiracy theories, he focused on staying scientific and showed a genuine curiosity about the mysteries that UFOs represented.

**4**
**Close Encounter of the First Kind**
The UFO is seen in close proximity.

**5**
**Close Encounter of the Second Kind**
The UFO has a physical effect, such as leaving marks or stopping car engines.

**6**
**Close Encounter of the Third Kind**
UFO occupants are seen in or around the craft.

> ABDUCTIONS

# THE TRAVIS WALTON INCIDENT

On the evening of 5th November 1975, lumber worker Travis Walton and six of his colleagues were driving through the forests of Snowflake, Arizona, USA. Upon seeing a UFO, the group pulled over to take a better look.

Walton stepped out of the truck and was apparently struck by a strange light, prompting his friends to pull away in blind panic. This marked the beginning of his five-day disappearance.

After fruitless searching by police and volunteers, Walton announced his 'return' in a call from a remote phone booth. The police believed the affair to be a hoax.

## Nordics and greys

When he returned, Walton explained that an alien abduction accounted for his disappearance. He recalled details of menacing greys, and his wanderings around the spaceship until he was returned to Earth by some kind Nordic aliens.

## Polygraph test

Walton took polygraph tests organised by the Aerial Phenomena Research Organization (APRO). He failed the first test but blamed the technician's rude behaviour for throwing the results. He then passed other tests, but polygraphs are now seen as unreliable for providing the truth.

The phone booth Walton phoned from after abduction

## Legacy in the media

Walton's story captivated the press and caught the public's attention due to his long disappearance and the witnesses to his abduction.

# IS BIGFOOT AN ALIEN?

The ape-like Bigfoot creature is an example of a cryptid, an animal whose existence is questionable. Those who specialise in the study of such mythic creatures are known as 'cryptozoologists'. Bigfoot has been the subject of sightings since the 19th century, while similar ape-like creatures have featured in folklore all over the planet.

Bigfoot crossed into the realm of UFOs in 1973, when witness Reafa Heitfield saw the creature enter a flying saucer outside her trailer home in Cincinnati, USA. Many cryptozoologists believe that cryptids might have a cosmic origin, either left behind on Earth or are the results of weird alien experiments.

## A quick cryptid guide

1. Hairy dwarf, Venezuela
2. Skunk ape, USA
3. Bigfoot, USA
4. Mongolian death worm, Gobi Desert
5. Batsquatch, USA
6. Pope Lick monster, USA
7. Yeti, Himalayan mountains
8. Ahool, Java
9. Crawfordville monster, USA
10. Gef the talking mongoose, UK
11. Dover demon, USA
12. Chupacabra, USA
13. Dogman, USA
14. Loveland frog, USA
15. Cabbagetown tunnel monster, USA
16. Jersey devil, USA
17. Spring-Heeled Jack, UK

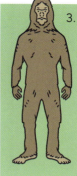

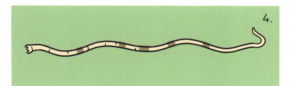

CLOSE ENCOUNTERS

# THE PETROZAVODSK INCIDENT

In the early hours of 20th September 1977, those around Petrozavodsk, USSR were treated to a brilliant UFO light display. The object took the form of a luminescent jellyfish that rained forth beams of light.

**Cold War worries**
According to journalists such as Nikolai Milov, some witnesses threw themselves under cover in terror, believing the display was the result of the long-dreaded nuclear apocalypse.

### Soaring satellite?

After widespread reportage, Sternberg Astronomical Institute researcher Lev Gindilis suggested that witnesses had simply seen the atmospheric effects of the Kosmos-955 satellite launch, which had taken place at a similar time.

Not everyone was satisfied, however, as critics noted that the UFO had the inclination to fly west, while Kosmos-955, like most rockets, was launched east (using the Earth's rotation as additional thrust).

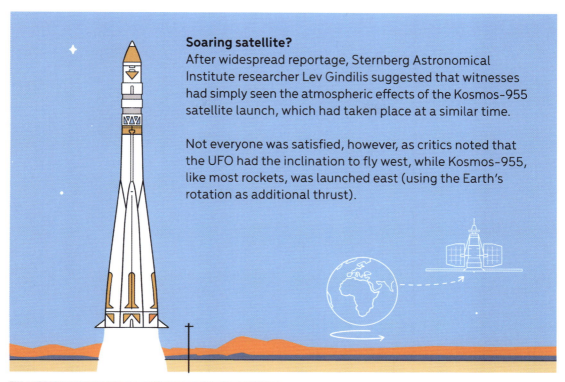

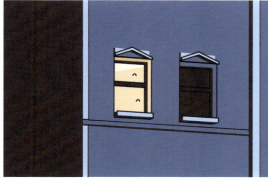

### Peculiar punctures

Some Petrozavodsk locals reported the appearance of coin-sized holes in windows during the incident.

It is possible, however, that these holes were already present and noticed only when residents intently peered through the glass to view the event.

### Curiosity killed the careers

The Soviet Institute of Sciences asked experts to look into the mystery. However, their investigation was unhelpful. One researcher, Vladimir Migulin, later admitted that many were hesitant because they feared damaging their reputations by getting involved in 'speculative science'.

# CROP CIRCLES

**'Crop circles'** are when corn fields are mysteriously flattened into circular patterns. They were a topic of interest by the start of the 80s, the era when films such as *E.T.* (1982) re-ignited interest in aliens. A handful of sightings of UFOs committing acts of crop vandalism solidified the phenomenon.

### Serious cereology
Investigators known as 'cereologists' specialised in the study of the phenomenon. At the peak of the craze, rural farms with new crop circles could expect a rush of cereologists, journalists and sightseers, all eager for access to the cryptic crops.

## Work of the Devil?

At the time they were first reported in 17th century England, many believed crop circles to be created by devils or færies. This was also the explanation for 'elf' or 'færie rings', the circular fungal growths that may be seen in grassy areas to this day.

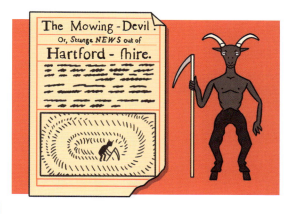

## Artists or aliens?

In 1991, artists Doug Bower and Dave Chorley announced that they were responsible for many of the crop circles around England since the late 1970s. In front of an eager audience of press and cereologists, they demonstrated how rope and wooden planks were used to make crop circles. There of course remains a stubborn group of those who believe it was UFOs.

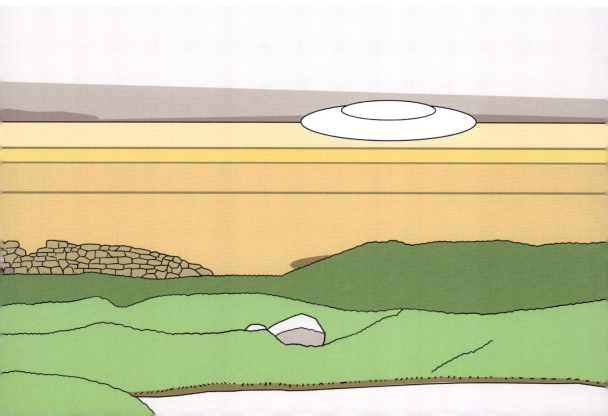

# THE 1980S

# CAUGHT ON CAMERA

The 1980s were perhaps the final era of widely shared UFO photos. As people grew suspicious of how easily visual effects could be faked, media coverage seemed to decrease. From the start, many UFO photos were exposed as fakes. Like ghost photography, tricks may be used to create convincing or poor quality paranormal documentation.

**Los Angeles, USA, 1942**
*This UFO was spotted by American anti-aircraft batteries and fired upon over the course of an hour. It was probably a stray balloon.*

**McMinville, Oregon, USA, 1950**
*Long considered genuine by many ufologists, skeptics believe the photo features a model hung by string.*

**Lossiemouth, UK, 1954**
*Likely copycat model of the 'Adamski-type' flying saucer.*

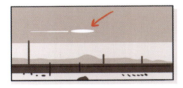

**Holloman Airforce Base, USA, 1957**
*A silver object. Project Blue Book judged the object to be a blurred image of an aeroplane.*

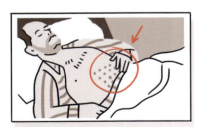

**Falcon Lake, Canada, 1967**
*Photo of Stefan Michalak's burn marks, which he claimed were inflicted by a flying saucer.*

**Burgh Marsh, UK, 1964**
*Apparently a space-suited alien, or more likely an effect of over-exposure.*

66

**Hessdalen, Norway, 1982,**
*A picture of the repeatedly documented local phenomena, judged to be some weird atmospheric event.*

**Gulf Breeze, USA, 1987**
*Almost certainly a model flying saucer, which was recently found in the attic of the photographer.*

**Ilkley, UK, 1987**
*A short alien on the Yorkshire moors. Skeptics say the object is a mannequin.*

**Wallonia, Belgium, 1990**
*A triangular spaceship, later revealed by the photographer to be made of polystyrene and light-bulbs.*

**Phoenix, Arizona, USA, 1997**
*A large triangular UFO, skeptics believe it to be an USAF flare exercise.*

**Antarctic, reported in 2018**
*A crashed flying saucer found on an internet map browser, or perhaps a chunk of rock that slipped down the mountain range.*

**La Junta, USA, 2019**
*Home security footage that seems to depict an alien or some type of færie. It is most likely a child with underwear on their head.*

**North Carolina Coast, USA, 2019**
*Footage of lights taken by a ferry passenger. Most likely a Navy flare exercise.*

CLOSE ENCOUNTERS

# THE RENDLESHAM FOREST INCIDENT

During Christmas 1980, the US Air Force base in Rendlesham, UK, was host to an unexpected festive guest. In the very early hours of Boxing Day, patrolling soldiers were astonished to discover a triangular craft parked in the woods.

The witness accounts vary, but one soldier felt the craft broadcast numbers directly into his mind, before whizzing off back into the sky. Returning later with police backup, the soldiers found broken branches and apparent landing marks on the ground.

## Extraterrestrial encore

Extraordinarily, the UFO came back that night. Elated soldiers interrupted Boxing Day dinner festivities to announce they had seen another light in the woods. A few soldiers hastily gathered an arsenal of recording equipment and went in pursuit.

While the soldiers have since given slightly differing accounts, they managed to observe unusual broken foliage and apparent heat traces of the object. Finally, in the early hours, they pursued a light above the tree-line. Remarkably, this chase was recorded on audio which captured the commentary of the soldiers as they observed the UFO's movements and bright colours before it disappeared.

Survey Meter

Tape recorder

## Just a lighthouse?

Prominent skeptic Ian Ridpath suggested the soldiers excitedly misinterpreted a range of nocturnal lights (a meteor, bright stars, and the nearby lighthouse) as a single event. Key witness John Burroughs has since admitted he had never seen the lighthouse before, suggesting they were unfamiliar with the landscape beyond their base.

# IN DEEP WATER

A tangent of ufology involves the study of **'Unidentified Submerged Objects' (USOs)**. These USOs have been documented for as long as there have been ships on the sea and range from sea monsters to flying saucers that launch out of the ocean.

**The Russian red sphere**
In 1965 the crew of the Soviet steamship *Raduga* was astonished to see a bright red sphere emerge from the sea some two miles from their ship. The sphere hovered above the waves, illuminating them with crimson light for several minutes before returning to the depths. Similar cases have been reported by ships throughout time. Some appear to be balls of light, while others have been described as solid silvery craft.

**Loch Ness monster**
The Loch Ness monster is a cryptid said to haunt the Loch Ness in Scotland. First appearing in the 19th century, it was later popularised in the 1930s by the famous 'Surgeon's photograph' which is now recognised as a forgery. Despite this, many have sworn to have encountered 'Nessie' and Loch Ness remains a popular tourist destination. Since the 1980s some ufologists have suggested that the Loch Ness monster is an abandoned alien or discarded hybrid experiment.

**Shag Harbour incident**
In 1967 at least eleven witnesses in rural Canada saw a UFO fall into the waters of Shag Harbour. Within 15 minutes of the crash Canadian police rowed out in an attempt to recover a floating object, only to watch it sink into frothing yellow foam. Military divers later attempted to recover the object but their efforts were unsuccessful. Like Loch Ness, Shag Harbour remains a paranormal tourist location.

**Fast Mover**
In 2017, ufologist Marc D'Antonio claimed to have been treated to a ride in a US Navy submarine, during which sonar operators got excited by a 'Fast Mover'. This is apparently the term for an unknown, underwater object travelling at high speed. At the time, the story was given significant attention in tabloid newspapers, but little confirmation has followed.

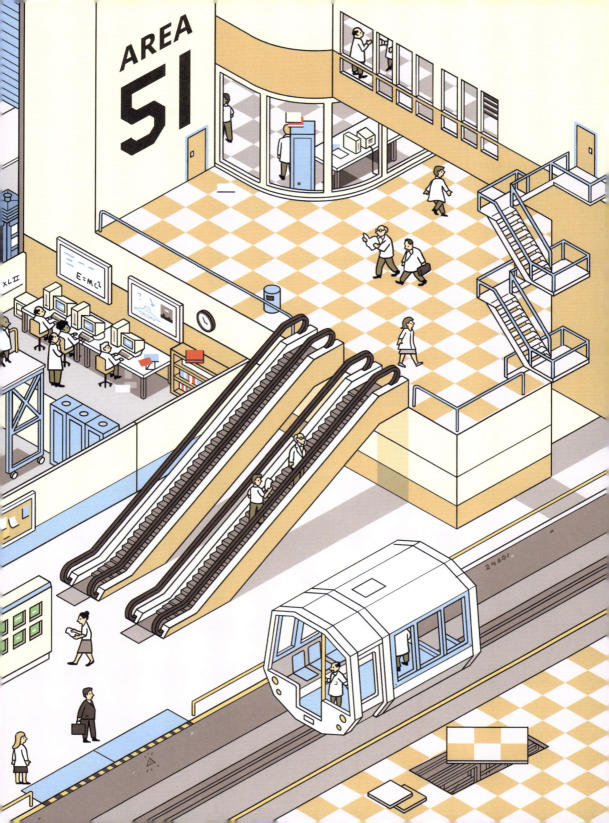

# AREA 51

Commonly known as **Area 51**, the USAF Groom Lake Facility in Nevada, USA is often associated with UFO conspiracies. In 1955, the base was established as a test facility for stealth aircraft and captured Soviet planes. Skeptics have suggested these tests may be the reason behind historic UFO sightings in the area.

### Weird whistle-blowers

In the 1980s individuals came forward claiming insider knowledge of government or military dealings with aliens. On 14th May 1989, Bob Lazar appeared as an informant on Las Vegas TV. Lazar revealed his work in back-engineering a flying saucer at the secret facility 'S4' near Area 51. According to Lazar, he was recruited after receiving prestigious degrees from MIT and Caltech.

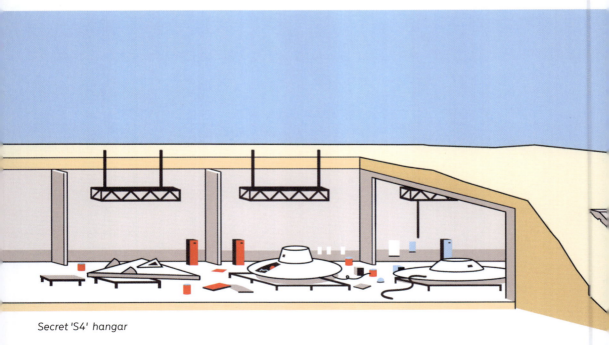

*Secret 'S4' hangar*

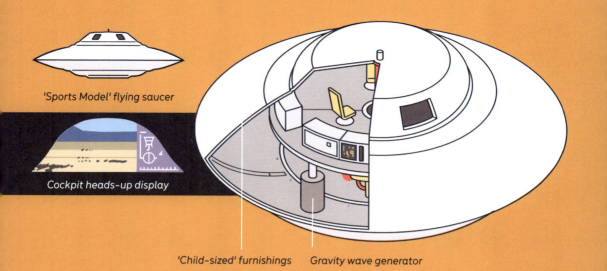

'Sports Model' flying saucer

Cockpit heads-up display

'Child-sized' furnishings  Gravity wave generator

## Sports Model
Lazar claimed his employment at S4 involved studying what he called the 'sports model' flying saucer (so named due to its sleek design). He also recalled briefing documents that made reference to the original owners of the craft: grey aliens from Zeta Reticuli.

### Friend or Fraud?
Ufologists such as Stanton Friedman called into question Lazar's academic background, for which they found no evidence. This led them to believe his tales of Area 51 were false. Around the year of 2000, many people came forward with strange claims, including some who even said they were time travellers, like a man called John Titor.

# THE 1990S

Lake Backsjön, Sweden, July 1999

# THE PHOENIX LIGHTS

On the night of 13th March 1997, residents around the state of Arizona witnessed two unusual events. The first event — shortly after 8pm — was described as a gigantic V-shaped craft with numerous lights drifting directly over Phoenix, Arizona, USA. The second event, around 10pm, involved nine lights that seemed to hover over Phoenix. This event was well-documented on video by onlookers.

Many witnesses were frustrated and unimpressed by the tone of reportage and the official explanations, and formed their own investigations and support groups. The Air Force claimed responsibility for the events, stating the lights had been flares dropped from an aircraft during a training exercise. Arizona's governor at the time, Fife Symington III, saw the funny side and held a press conference in where one of his staff members dressed up in an alien costume.

The Phoenix lights are perhaps the best-documented contemporary mass-UFO sighting, a reminder that UFO witnesses are usually ordinary people.

# 21ST CENTURY

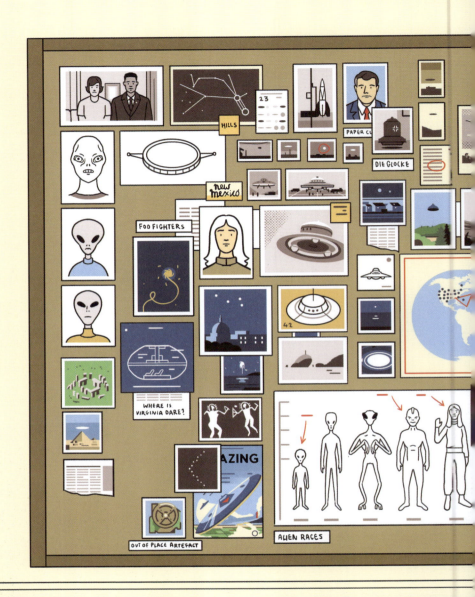

# GOVERNMENT DISCLOSURE

Today, many ufologists believe their most important work is pushing for the government to release official UFO information. They hope that this will reduce the ridicule surrounding UFOs and encourage more experienced scientists to take it seriously.

With fewer new UFO sightings, ufologists have shifted their focus to paranoid government conspiracy theories instead.

A large UFO enthusiast conference

Small public event

Podcast

Online expert

## Hack the planet

In 2002, Scottish UFO enthusiast Gary McKinnon was arrested on suspicion of hacking into US military computers and causing unlawful damage. McKinnon said that his motive was to find secret UFO evidence. He has given interviews about the secret files he claims to have seen, including pictures of UFOs and suspicious spreadsheets.

## Memes and clickbait

Online UFO culture is often the subject of low quality clickbait and ironic humour.

## The Area 51 raid

On 20th September 2019, a large group of people arrived at Area 51 to, quote, "see them aliens". The raiders took pictures and enjoyed a spontaneous music festival. Unfortunately, they were unable to release any alien prisoners.

# THE PENTAGON'S SAUCER SEARCH

The US's intelligence headquarters, known as the Pentagon, began the Advanced Aerospace Threat Identification Program (AATIP) in 2007. The purpose of this project was to study **'Unidentified Aerial Phenomena' (UAP)**, a new label for UFOs.

The program was revealed in 2017, when footage of UFOs tracked by Navy jets was leaked. Officials confirmed the validity of the videos in 2020.

Luis Elizondo, AATIP Director 2007–2012

### The USS Nimitz incident
In November 2004, the US Navy tracked a UFO off the coast of California. Two Super Hornet jets from the USS Nimitz were sent to intercept. The pilots were startled to discover a white oblong-shaped UFO hovering above churning waves. Thankfully, they were able to record their pursuit of the object on their infrared cameras.

## Excessive acronyms

The US intelligence community is made up of agencies and outside helpers. AATIP gave a research job to a company called Bigelow Aerospace Advanced Space Studies (BAASS). The owner, Robert Bigelow, caught the attention of Pentagon by talking about his allegedly haunted property, known as 'Skinwalker Ranch'.

## Whispered work

While it was reported that AATIP closed down in 2012, insiders say that it is still running in some form. The Pentagon avoids giving clear answers when journalists ask about it.

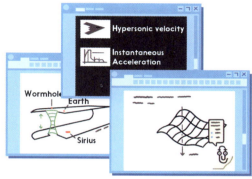

# SETI

The Search for Extraterrestrial Intelligence (SETI) is the collective effort of many scientists who track different signals from space and look for any that seem more coherent than random background noise. Many believe that if we find proof of alien life, it will come from a radio telescope, not a flying saucer landing in front of a surprised world leader.

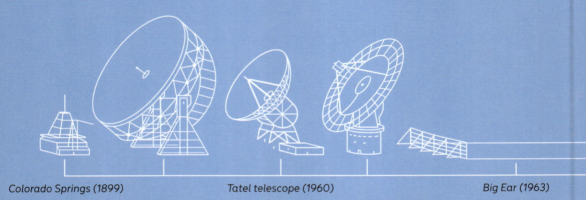

Colorado Springs (1899)  Tatel telescope (1960)  Big Ear (1963)
Jodrell Bank (1957)  Parkes Observatory (1961)

**Talking to extraterrestrials**

Humanity has also made efforts to send messages to alien races, should they be watching and listening. Other than broadcasting radio signals, space satellites have been equipped with illustrative plaques just in case aliens miraculously understand human symbols. During SETI operations, some interesting radio signals have been picked up, like the famous 'Wow!' signal in 1977, named because the scientist who saw it wrote 'Wow!' on the print-out.

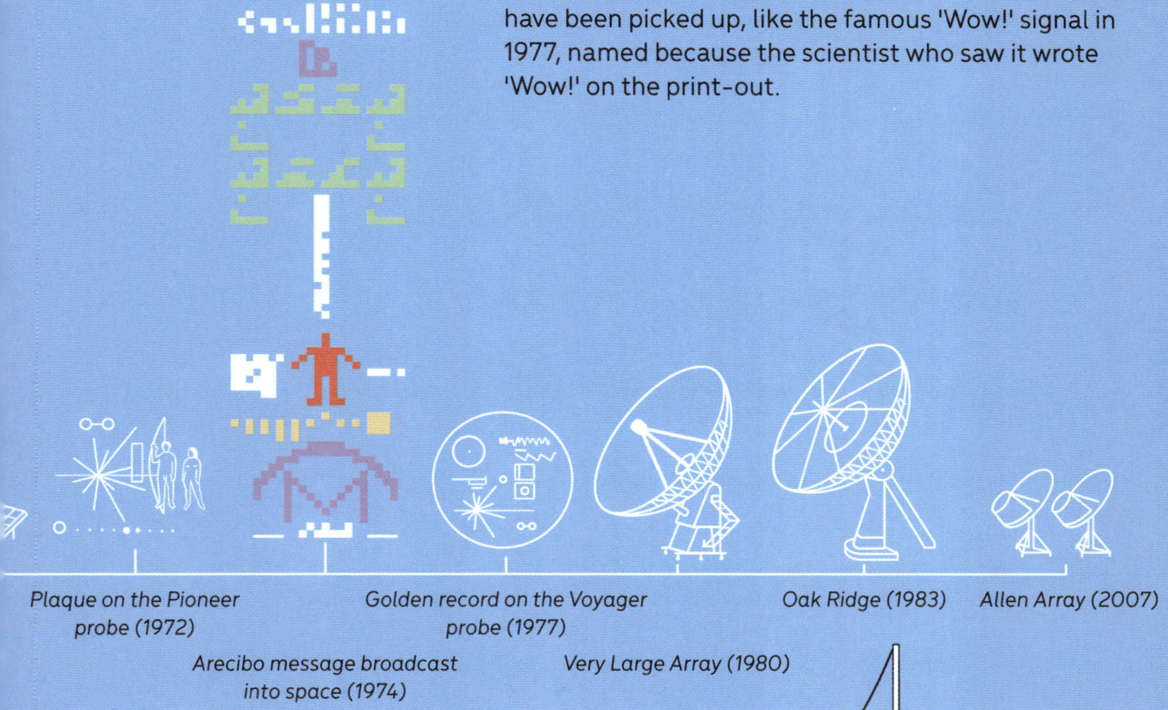

Plaque on the Pioneer probe (1972)

Arecibo message broadcast into space (1974)

Golden record on the Voyager probe (1977)

Very Large Array (1980)

Oak Ridge (1983)

Allen Array (2007)

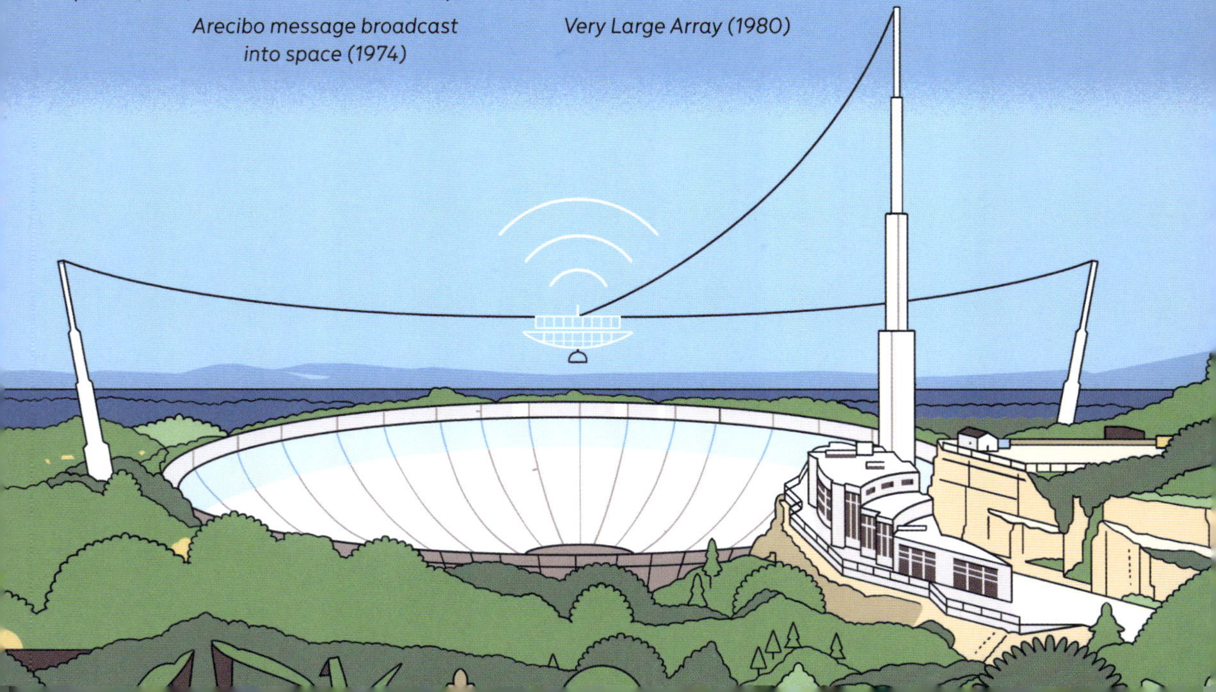

# UFOLOGY TODAY

The interest in UFOs and ufology continues thanks to the contributions of investigators, books, conferences, conventions, forums, podcasts, popular culture and a mass of online experts.

The study of UFOs is a practice full of passionate and colourful individuals. Certainly, it takes a degree of courage and dedication to investigate a topic so full of complex stories and strange details.

Some critics believe the study of UFOs peaked years ago with government projects like Project Blue Book. They argue that research has declined and that it has shifted into a focus on conspiracy theories.

There are large amounts of new UFO cases every year.

Rather than concluding with the boring, vague phrase, 'we may never know,' I shall instead issue the following advice: watch the skies and for goodness' sake bring a good camera.

# GLOSSARY

**Abductee**
Person who claims to have been taken by UFO occupants.

**Area 51**
United States Air Force base. Some associate the base with the testing of recovered UFOs and other spooky activities.

**Cold War**
The Cold War was a conflict between the United States and the Soviet Union from the end of the Second World War to the early 1990s. They didn't fight directly but competed in many ways, like trying to have the best weapons and space missions.

**Contactee**
Person who claims to have either met or had telepathic communication with extraterrestrial beings.

**Crop circle**
Crops flattened into creative patterns, usually attributed to inventive artists and pranksters.

**Foo Fighter**
Small, bright UFOs, witnessed around planes during the Second World War.

**Flap**
Large increase in UFO sightings, usually because of a well-reported event.

**Flying saucer**
Description applied to UFOs, commonly used since Kenneth Arnold's sighting in 1947 above Mt. Rainer.

**Grey**
Alien being, commonly reported in sightings and by abductees.

**Hynek Scale**
Professor J. Allen Hynek's method of classifying UFO witness statements. Statements are sorted into close encounters of the first, second or third kind.

**Mass hysteria**
Group panic based on fear, producing collective illusions and obsessive behaviour.

**Megalith**
Large stones that were used to create structures and monuments like the famous Stonehenge in Wiltshire, UK.

**Men in Black**
Malevolent agents that reportedly stalk, threaten or question folk who have seen a UFO. Commonly initialised as 'MiB'.

**Missing time**
Experience where abductees have reported gaps in memory, in which hours or even days may pass unaccounted-for.

**RADAR**
Acronym for 'RAdio Detection And Ranging'; a system for detecting objects by broadcasting radio waves. The waves that are reflected back are interpreted to determine the size and speed of objects.

**Skeptic**
Person who values scientific inquiry. They don't believe something right away and want proof before deciding if it's true.

**Sleep paralysis**
Common explanation for abduction experiences, in which folk are unable to move and experience fear and hallucinations when falling asleep or waking up.

**Swamp gas**
Natural gasses produced by rotting vegetation. The gasses occasionally produce flying fireballs, which may explain various UFO sightings.

**Spooklight**
Anomalous light that reappears in the same location. Explanations offered tend to involve aircraft or car headlights.

**UAP**
Unidentified Aerial Phenomena – the modern term for 'UFO' preferred by US officials.

**UFO**
Initialism for 'Unidentified Flying Object'. Refers to any unrecognised thing in the sky.

**Ufologist**
Investigator or student of UFO phenomena.

**USO**
Initialism for 'Unidentified Submerged Object'. Refers to peculiar and unrecognised objects underwater.

**Weather balloon**
Explanation for various UFO sightings and crashes; including the Roswell incident in 1947.

    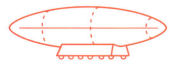

# INDEX

## A

AATIP 84–5
abductions by aliens 15, 44, 50, 56–7
  Betty and Barney Hill 44–5
  Travis Walton 56–7
Adamski, George 36–7
airships, mystery 18
Andreasson, Betty 44–5
Antikythera mechanism 13
Anunnaki 14
APRO 57
Area 51 72–5, 83
Arnold, Kenneth 24–6
Atlantis 32
Azteks 13

## B

BAASS 85
Barker, Gray 28
Berlitz, Charles 26
Bermuda Triangle 32–3
Bigelow, Robert 85
Bigfoot 58–9
Bower, Doug 63
Brazel, William 'Mac' 26-7
BUFORA 49

## C

*Carroll A. Deering* 33
cave paintings 13
CBS 20–1
cereologists 62
Chorley, Dave 63
CIA 31
civilian UFO associations 48–9
Cold War 47, 60
crop circles 62–3
Crowley, Aleister 17
cryptids 58–9
cryptozoologists 58
CUFOS 31

## D

Däniken, Erich Von 12
D'Antonio, Marc 71
daylight discs 54
devils 63
Drury Affair 39

## E

Egyptian pyramids 1–3

## F

færies 14–5, 32, 63
Fast Mover 71
'The Father Gill Sighting' 39
Finland 15
flying saucers 24–5, 30, 36, 75
  Adamski Type 36–7
  Travis Walton incident 56–7
Foo fighters 19
Friedman, Stanton 75

## G

Gernon, Bruce 33
Giant Rock Spacecraft Convention 40–1
god-aliens, Middle Eastern 14
government disclosure 39, 82–3
green children 15
grey aliens 17, 46, 57

## H

Hessdalen lights 67
Hill, Betty and Barney 44–5
Houdini, Harry 17
Hynek, Professor J. Allen 31, 54–5
Hynek scale 54–5

## I

identified flying objects 46–7
the Integratron 41
iron pillar, India 13

## J

Jessup, M.K. 32

## K

Kean, Leslie 50
Kecksburg Incident 50-1
Keyhoe, Major Donald 45
Kosmos-955 satellite 61

## L

La Viesta, Vesta 16
Lam 17
Lazar, Bob 74–5
Loch Ness monster 70

## M

McKinnon, Gary 83
Martians 16, 20–1
Maury Island 25
mediums 16–7, 36
megaliths 12
Men in Black (MiB) 28–9
Michalak, Stefan 66
Middle Eastern god-aliens 14
Moai, Easter Island 13
Moore, William 26
MUFON 49

## N

NASA 50
Nazca lines, Peru 12–3
Nibiru 14
NICAP 45, 49
*Nimitz, USS* 84
Nordics 36, 57

## O

Orthon 36
Ouija boards 17

## P

Palmer, Raymond 24–5
Pease Airforce Base 45
Pentagon 84–5
petroglyphs 12–3
Petrozavodsk incident 60–1
Phoenix lights 78–9
Project Blue Book 30–1, 36, 46, 54, 66
Project Grudge 30
'Project Mogul' 27
Project Sign 30

## Q

Quimbaya artefact 13

## R

Raduga 70
Rendlesham Forest incident 68–9
Robertson Panel 31
Roswell Army Air Field (RAAF) 26
Roswell Incident 26–7
Royal Australian Airforce (RAAF) 38

## S

St. Elmo's fire 19
Saucer Clubs 49
Second World War 19
SETI 86–7
Shakoki-dogu figurine 13
Shaver, Richard 24–5
Sitchin, Zecharia 14
Soviet Institute of Sciences 61
Space Brothers 36–7
space satellites 87
Spencer, John 32
spiritualism 16
sports model flying saucer 75
Sternberg Astronomical Institute 61
Stonehenge, UK 13
Surgeon's photograph 70
swamp gas 15, 46

## T

Titor, John 75

## U

ufologists 8
UFOs: common shapes 9
  origin of term 24
  through time 2–3, 94–5
UAP 84
USOs 70
US Air Force (USAF) 8, 46, 68
  415th Night Fighter Squadron 19
  Groom Lake Facility 74–5
  Project Blue Book 30–1, 36, 46, 54, 66
Rendlesham Forest incident 68–9
US Navy 33, 71, 84
USSR 60

## V

Van Tassel, George 40–1
Verne, Jules 18
Vikings 12

## W

Walton, Travis 56–7
Welles, Orson 20
Wells, H.G. 18, 20–1
will-o'-the-wisps 15
Willoughby, Richard 15
Woolpit 15

## Z

Zeta Reticuli 75
Zimbabwe 95

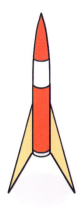

# UFOS THROUGH TIME

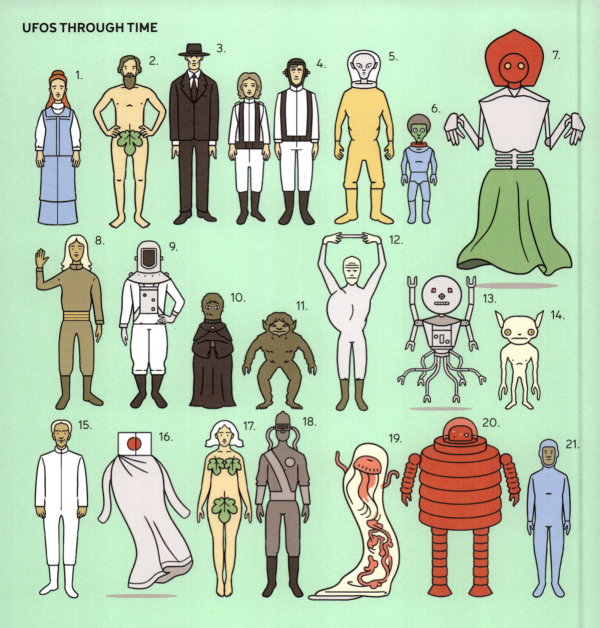

1. Hitachi Province, Japan (1803)
2. Springfield, MI, USA (1896)
3. Man in Black (1940s–present)
4. Ängelholm, Sweden (1946)
5. Bauru, Brazil (1947)
6. Villa Santina, Italy (1947)
7. Flatwoods, WV, USA (1952)
8. Colorado Desert, CA, USA (1952)
9. Hasselbach, Germany (1952)
10. Moselle, France (1954)
11. Carcass, Venezuela (1954)
12. Branch Hill, OH, USA (1955)
13. Riverside, CA, USA (1955)
14. Hopkinsville, KY, USA, (1955)
15. Drakensburg, S. Africa (1956)
16. Old Say Brook, CA, USA (1957)
17. Minas Gerias, Brazil (1957)
18. Minas Gerias, Brazil (1957)
19. Domesten, Sweden (1958)
20. Cãdiz, Spain (1960)
21. Eagle River, WI, USA (1961)
22. Lancaster, NH (1962)
23. Felixstowe, UK (1965)
24. Point Pleasant, WV, USA (1966)

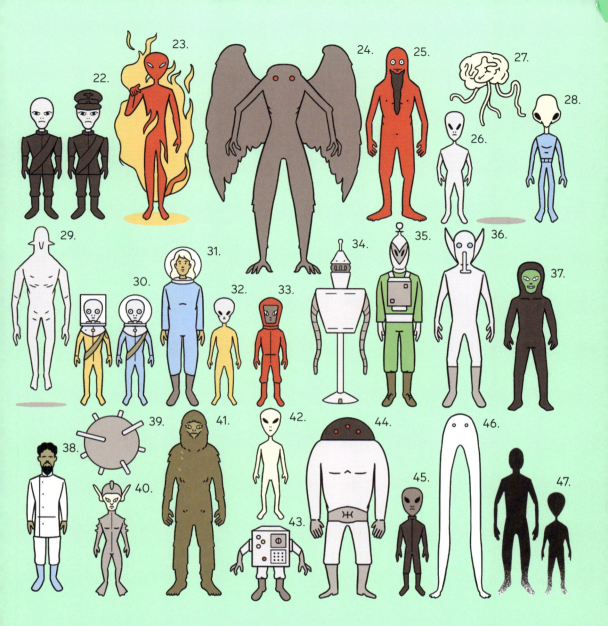

25. Coleraine, Canada (1968)
26. Cussac, France (1967)
27. Palos Verdas, CA, USA (1971.
28. Allagash, ME, USA (1972)
29. Pascagoula, MI, USA (1973)
30. Warneaton, Belgium (1974)
31. Snowflake, AZ, USA (1975)
32. Snowflake, AZ, USA (1975)
33. The Canary Islands (1976)
34. Paciendia, Brazil (1977)
35. Puerto Rico (1977)
36. Samaya, Japan (1978)
37. Emilcin, Poland (1978)
38. Mindalore, S. Africa (1979)
39. Dechmont, UK (1979)
40. Puerto Rico (1980)
41. Mt. Mernon, MI, USA (1983)
42. Upstate NY, USA (1985)
43. Voronezh, Russia (1989)
44. Voronezh, Russia (1989)
45. Ruwa, Zimbabwe (1994)
46. Fresno, CA (2010)
47. Shadow entities (present)